RIGGER

&

HOIST

ANOTHER

poems by

Laura McCullough

BLACK LAWRENCE PRESS

Black Lawrence Press
www.blacklawrence.com

Executive Editor: Diane Goettel
Book Design: Mary Austin Speaker
Cover Design: Mary Austin Speaker

Copyright © 2013 Laura McCullough
ISBN: 978-1-937854-29-4

Black Lawrence Press
326 Bigham Street
Pittsburgh, PA 15211

Published 2013 by Black Lawrence Press, an imprint of Dzanc Books.
Printed in the United States

BOOKS BY LAURA MCCULLOUGH

Panic

Speech Acts

What Men Want

The Dancing Bear

For Mandee

CONTENTS

I

MEMBRANE

II

DANDELIONS

III

THE DOOR

ACKNOWLEDGMENTS

Grateful acknowledgment to all the editors who published these poems, sometimes in earlier forms or under other titles.

The American Poetry Review "Dispensable," "At the Combine: Threshing," "You May Think I am Suggesting Women are the 'Gentler Sex,'" and "There were Only Dandelions

Green Mountains Review "' Well, Clarice, have the lambs stopped screaming?'" and "Scarification" as "The Door"

Diode Magazine "Arrogance," "Lighter," "A Kind of Apology," as "Bob at the Corner Table of the Lincroft Inn," "Progenitors of the New Whale," and "The Dog is Lying at My Feet as I Write this Poem"

Iron Horse Literary Review "Like Water on Pavement"

Fourteen Hills "Fomentation" as "Making"

Sweet "Blessed Knife"

Burnside Review "Rigger Death and Hoist Another"

Spoon River "A Girl's Shaved Head"

The Literary Review "Queerness Means Questioning the Mythical Norms" as "God is Queer"

Southern Indiana Review "He Says the Sins"

The New Ohio Review "Fall and I Talk" as "Spring Cleaning"

Gutter Eloquence Magazine "This is Not an Audition"

FRiGG "And Some Join the Military," "Through a Break" as "When I Was Growing Up," and "Possession" as "My Daughter Lost Her First Tooth Today"

Oranges and Sardines: Poets and Artists "The Cave," "Trajectory," "What We Want," "Beauty Salon Love," "So Does She Get The Dog Or Not?," "Evanescence," "So It's The End of The World Again," and "God On The Ropes"

Contrary Magazine "They Dream of AK47s"

The DMQ Review "Knowledge"

Riverbabble "To the God of Pyrography" and "The Small God of Winter; a Little God of Temperatures"

South Jersey Underground "Saturation" and "In Physics Radiation Describes"

Scythe "What Foolishness" and "You Might Say This is Not a Poem"

Redactions: Poetry & Poetics, "Those Things Outside"

Referential "When Wonder," "Longing," and "The Lips were the Worst" "What Really Dies in Autumn" appeared at From the Fishouse: an audio archive of emerging poets.

"What We Want" and "Beauty Salon Love" appeared in the anthology, *The Girl With Red Hair.*

"The Flags We Raise" appeared on Poets on Adoption.

Thank you to Laure-Anne Bosselaar, Kurt Brown, Stephen Dunn, Jeffrey Ford, Kathleen Graber, Mihaela Moscaliuc, R. Dwayne Betts, Mark Halliday, Tony Hoagland, Peter Murphy (and his amazing Winter Poetry & Prose Getaway), Suzanne Parker, and Michael Waters for various support, feedback, and advice, and to the Sewanee Writers Conference where this manuscript was brought to completion. Thank you to Mary Austin Speaker, terrific book designer and writer, as well. Thank you to Diane Goettel, thoughtful and sharp editor with big dreams and a willingness to help others with theirs. And to Michael Broek, there aren't enough thanks to suffice.

All I know is a door into the dark.

SEAMUS HEANEY

The day of the absolute is over, and we're in for the strange gods once more.

DH LAWRENCE

If trees could speak, they wouldn't.

DORIANNE LAUX

I

MEMBRANE

TRAJECTORY

Here we are not whisked away to jail
    in the middle of the night;
    instead we are ignored,
    or perhaps that's too generous
    implying some awareness;
    rather it is as if we are invisible,
    no star or scar or color or accent,
    nothing to reveal us except the odd comment
    at the Little League game,
    the Foundation fund-raising dinner.   No one
    pulls us over and demands   *anything!*

It is as if we have fallen into the collective amnesia
    of the world: too busy
        keeping on all the lights
        against the encroaching dark
        or standing in line at the pharmacy
        watching the lions on TV
        eating each other endlessly.

Who stole humor?   God
    is buried under the floor
    of the Mall of America
    below the roller-coaster.

Is this is why we cut off pieces of ourselves
    or withhold food,
    or get tattoos, that invasion
    of skin by small, sharp instruments?

There, that little pain again—
    is it all we know to offer?   See
    that field?   The nest of baby rabbits?

    That rototiller with the hobby farmer behind it?

At the Black Abbot on High Street,
    drinking single malt—it was Scotland,
    a minute's walk to the North Sea—
    the guy next to me might have felt
    he was a cliché, too, just back
    from a three week stint on an oil rig
    starting his fourteen days home,
    divorced, and on his own.

He was a crane operator
    and wore small round glasses on his boney,
    bent nose, looking at me over the rim,
    grinning with a loose mouth, teeth askew
    and talked fast, showing me his tattoos:
        inside his lower lip: MOM;
        an oilman's cartoon on his shoulder;
        a sun on his belly;
        and only joked about the two trees
        flanking his groin
        "to make me penis look larger," he said.
    How could I not be won over? And clinked glasses,
    cheered with him as if I knew where I was
    and what I was doing there.

It took a month after the Gulf Coast rig blew
    for me to think of that guy,   to wish
    I'd kissed the coin he'd tossed in the air—:
    heads, I'd stay; tails, go—had done something
        besides laugh.

Now, I think of the trees on his thighs
    I don't really believe existed,
    but mostly of his good humor,
    what a fine time he gave me, a girl
    on the loose in a town bar in a far town
    glad to be disassembled from the rigging

of her own life.   What matter
that all he wanted was connection,
to recover from weeks of living
above water, off hoisting things
from one place to another?   Scotch

whisky's smoke comes from peat.   *Mouth feel*
relies on the size and shape of the stills.
Oil is distilled, too, as are memories,
each time retold, re-shaped as the bangs
and nicks of mind change,   the mind
a kind of still, as well,   and each time we tell
something, we burn   the way peat is burned,
details like smoke added back to the kiln
increasing the flavor.   Still, it took me
a while to recall my rigger, tatted and grimy
though he smelled of soap.   Did he?
I can't quite recall, and did anyone die
in the Gulf Coast disaster? Yes, of course—
eleven—but I never met any of them.

Peat has many uses: it stabilizes flood zones,
amends soil, can be cooked on, warmed by,
but is dangerous when left unattended,
can catch fire,   like oil
which comes from similar basic matter:
things that have lived and then died.

Peat on the tongue is hard to describe,
like a memory that won't quite latch,
there at the back of the mind's throat,
green in its darkest hue settling inside
your chest.   Maybe this is why bodies
are so often buried there: 700 bog men
have been recovered.   My nameless rigger
is not a bog man; the eleven in the Gulf
died, some just missing, blogs, replacing bodies,
repeating the same words: *so sorry, loss, responsibility.*

The North Sea is connected to the Gulf Coast
        by so many miles of water   my mind
        can not contain any of it.   When I left my rigger
        at the bar, his coin having failed him,
        I stood a little drunk on the beach
        picking up small stones I could carry
        home in just a pocket, pebbles, really,
        greens and reds that puddle now in a small dish
        on my desk, maybe a hundred, like tiny eggs.

Is this what we resort to?
        Organic souvenirs, hidden honeys, seeds
        and plants we smuggle from the places
        we've been? Why we plant our children's
        lost teeth in the garden, sift death-ashes
        into rivers and oceans, stand on the edge
        of wide water facing it, or rowing over it
        or churning below it, or building platforms
        above it, as if we might claim some control

        and maybe why we drink, why we pay
        for the rarest malts, the most smoke
        and wood,

        why we hoist another one, nosing and tasting,
        taking sips and rolling our lost
        histories around the tongue, so they penetrate—
        and distill—
        the scarred membranes
        hidden inside our mouths.

SO IT'S THE END OF THE WORLD   AGAIN

The world is coming to an end,
     the Mayan calendar says,
     which is not what scholars of such things say it says,
     but which a filmmaker made good use of
     to show us what the world coming to an end
     might look like if we could see in hyper-realistic terms
     over and over and in the kind of detail
          real humans
          in real crisis
          can not see.

Then, when the world is crashing,
     when the meta-narrative metaphors
     the world's monuments represent
     are bashed and smashed,
     we would not see,   but only feel,
     the lens of us not enlarging
     but growing smaller and smaller still,
     reduced to the size of a little girl

     cowering behind a bed   in a corner.

The news report says a video shows
     the girl being carried into the hotel room
     by a man not her father for purposes
     of "sexual servitude," and her mother
     is charged with prostitution
     and making false statements
     to the police for telling them
     the girl was missing
     when in fact, she'd sold her.

Everything the girl believed in—
        without knowing
        she was doing something
        called "believing in"—
        has been broken into and ransacked,

and she is so small,
        and all she knows to be true
        is the only thing that's true:
a monster moves towards her
        in slow motion
        with hands so big,
        there's nothing she can do
        but close her eyes.

THROUGH A BREAK

We always took the same route to the candy store,
      the shorter one our parents didn't tell us about:
      going up a side street
      to the gravel parking lot
      behind the Golden Eagle Bar
      through a break in the fence.

I never saw anyone come out the bar's back door,
      not even when it was open
      like it was all summer,
      and you could see a dark humid space
      with huddled shapes and blisters of light,
      but one day we found
      a dead cat in the gravel by the fence.

            With a stick poked up its ass
                and one through the neck.

You know what a dead cat looks like:
      matted, dusty, stiff.
        Just a dead cat
            with a stick up its ass.

I was not exactly afraid.   It was the summer

      we all talked   about the kid
      who had to go to the hospital
          because a teenager had hammered
             a nail into his skull;
     the summer two kids got washed
          into an overflow pipe
             during a downpour and drowned;

the summer we all stopped at the creek
    one day on the way to the candy store
        and climbed inside that storm drain

to show each other our *private parts*
as if we could actually reveal what was happening to us.

POSSESSION

Once, I knew a child with only one eye
    named David who had leukemia.
His uncle built him a working train in the backyard
    of his fancy and well landscaped house.
Sometimes all of us kids would be invited to ride it.

He was dead before we were all twelve.

There was that experiment in science class,
    where a cut stem white flower
    is set into a vial of colored liquid.   Like dye
for Easter eggs. The flower absorbs it;
    the petals are infused. The cells have all been penetrated.
      Purple   *Magenta*   *Cerulean*

[Stephen says he hates those who use words like cerulean.
Sometimes a sky is just gray.   Just a sky.]

A tooth is a milestone. *I am getting big*, my daughter exclaims!

The Pearl-bordered Fritillary is an early spring butterfly
    that depends upon dandelions for nectar.

I've always buried my children's teeth in the garden.

    A tooth can not be just a tooth.
    It is sky.
    It is wooden wheels.
    It is the sins of the fathers.
    It is dreaming of money.
    It is no money to give
        and the neighbor's car repossessed in the night,
        all of us awakened by the tow truck,   the hammer-lock,
        the dumb stare of humiliated denial;
        no more sleep tonight for the adults,
        just the children who will wake early,

look to see if the Tooth Fairy left money,
excited because the neighbor's children
will ride with us to school today,
    piled in the back
    like people used to do.

FALL AND I TALK

When we moved the couch
    we found the pumpkin,
    the tiny one we'd picked that day in the run-up to Halloween
    with the kids at the apple-picking farm.
It was small to begin with, smaller than an apple,
    and now it is desiccated
    though not as much as you might imagine;
its top-sunken and wrinkled, the bottom flatter,
    but the whole of it soft
    as if it might be full of rot or even of crème,
    as if you might pry it open
    along one of the long wrinkles or fissures,
    that autumn orange color gone pale,
    and out might come some wonderful and unexpected thing.

I don't pry it open, but can't bear to throw it out.
Instead I place it by the little handle of its stem onto the mantel.
    It is happy there, and I too feel happy,
    a little survivor, not blazing,
    but brilliant in my still-here-ness,
    a bit proud of myself.
In spring I can never remember fall,
    and I talk myself through the laughing-at-you days of spring
    that never deliver what they promise.
    Only July gives you everything.
    Then August begins to take it away.
    And there's not enough to lose anymore.

Which is why we always pick so many more apples
    than we could ever eat, bags and bags full,
    and why so many will go bad,
    that sticky odor coming up from the produce drawer,
    the ooze that always gets on your hand
    when you reach in without looking.

LANGUAGE, DUMB

In linguistics, binding theory is any of a broad class of theories dealing with the distribution of pronominal and anaphoric elements.

She said,
> *I love you, I love you, I love you, I love you, I love you, I love you, I do.*
And I thought, maybe I have to rethink
> my negative relationship with anaphora,
> which is more complex than simple repetition might suggest,
> but if we forgo a discussion of syntax,
> and agree that order and rules are important,
> and also agree that we *should* argue about semantics,
> does that leave us in any better condition?

Or should I simply, listen. Listen as she says
> this, again,
IloveyouIloveyouIloveyouIloveyouIloveyouIloveyouIdo,

> and for the moment that moves beyond the annoyance
> of simple repetition in the intellect
> and becomes a small collection of spit in the throat
> that must be swallowed

which is only a symptom of feeling,
> of some switch in the neural net of the organ called my brain
> and I hear, as Frost said,   not as a barbarian,
> but even more elementally,   and *I love you*
> becomes not words,
> or merely sound,
> but a conveyance across which something is exchanged,

> and a spoke in the wheel of me is lit up.
> > *I love youIloveyouIdo,* my darling, my dear one,

> grateful to stand on the rules of language
> that are the architecture of this cathedral
> upon the roof of which we now stand,

bound to each other by nothing less permanent   than language,
dumb monkeys that we are,

gripping each other for dear life
and always so ready to leap.

LONGING

It's there inside each moment, molecule,
in the lining of the clothes she folds,
in the lint she pulls from the dryer's lip;
she feels it in the marks along her arms,
the threads of Alice and Dorothy, amputated
myths she once loved. *Little Red* in red
script across her lower back; *tramp stamp*,
her mother calls it. *Tramp stamp*, she says,
behind her mother's back, *oh my yes*,
and behind the neck, one small star broken
into shards and drops of blood that shift
from magenta to purple to green and then
white, down along her ribs—they hurt—
and this small half moon on the cusp
of her thumb and forefinger, how it folds
when she closes her hand as she folds clothes,
her boyfriend's shirt, the ravaged one he uses
to work out in, the arms cut off and the neck
slit; she folds and unfolds it again, the moon
rueful in the crease shutting down, now
opening, gone, there again, blue.

WHEN WONDER

There on the hood of the dryer, all hum
and heat, legs folded, she sits like rebar
as if waiting for cement to rain down.
What thrums underneath is all that's keeping
her alive, that and the corona around her
head that her boyfriend sees when he squints.

All this sound, this thrashing, rises around
her silencing the ache between her ears.
For a moment, she can be still. On the street
with his cigarette, he watches through the window,
the close to silent air humming about his head.

They bled ink for days, and couldn't be kissed;
she could barely eat. Swollen like small plum slices,
she was afraid for a little while, but then it
was alright. He kissed her one night, just on the corner
because he was afraid though he had not told her
so. He touched a finger to the bottom one and then checked;
they were set. *What do you think now*, he asked her,
and she pouted. *My eyes*, she said, *I'll do them next*. He
blinked. *I don't think I could do my eyes*, he said.
She touched the small nob of metal between his eyes. *You
did this*, she said. *That's different*, he said. *That's
the bullet I've dodged my whole life. Bang, Quentin Tarantino
to the head*. He ran his pinky across his lashes
letting them feather across his skin. He touched the lid. *This*,
he said, *is baby flesh*. He moved to touch hers, but
she startled away from him, covering her face, looking
at him through the bars of her black tipped fingers.

WHAT WE WANT

The mortician knows his job,   makes his money;
      we all want to look lovely in the end,
      or at least used up,
      like we took the ride as far as it would go,
         got out,   and jumped.

This poem in my belly makes me nauseous
      as chemicals hit
      the chemicals we are—
      which ones will kill, which ones save?

It's all an empty sky, but your hair looks better
      than it did when you were alive,
      and someone sighs,
      Do you think she just had good bones, to look so good?

Thin threads holding it all together—
      we whisperers in the corner, praisers
      of the makeup, sewn lips and lids.

I wish he'd do me, someone else says,
      snickers from the teenager
      who doesn't get any of this
      and doesn't understand she can wear her hair
         any which way,
             dress in paper bags,
                and her age would make her radiant.

We close in around her, oh, we know it;   we want it;
      we touch her hair,
      take the strand she is sucking on from her lips.
      Your time will come, we smile;
      we smile in the empty air
      we shape into poems
      reclaiming fear,
         meanness much easier to stand

and our eyes turning red
    reveal everything we wish
        we could say, but can not.

GIRL'S HEAD SHAVED

To promote thicker hair.

To prevent lice.

As an offering to god, gods,   the gods of lice
        and men.
And it was hot, more than most of us
        can stand, and it made sense, this shearing,
        and there she was with the secret bones
        of her skull revealed, everything
        about her future listed in the shades
        of stubble, lying face down across
        the knee of a nurse or nun, whomever
        it was, nothing to hide her face behind,
        the eyes of someone who understands
        the body is always sacrificial.

        Prostrated to everything.

It always grows back.   Weeds
        overrunning the temple.

See her now, beautiful

        and infested.

BEAUTY SALON LOVE

He says, *Oh, I understand your hair; you need...*
  and rattles off a litany that includes
  coconut oil infusion
  after, of course, a clarifying shampoo,
  and talks curl shape and cuticle health
  and color, *Oh, we'll talk color next time;*
    your red is so good, we don't need to go there yet,
    but when we do, you're in the right hands,

and I admit, I started to weep,
  not a lot, but yes, like when you've finally made love
  rather than had sex,
  the whole sweep of your future
  opening both out to that future
  and back to the dream
  you had as a little girl of being rescued
  and loved for ever and ever and ever

and suddenly I could make love to my new hair-guy,
  but instead buy close to two hundred dollars worth of products,
  everything he says will transform me,
  and I nod as he takes my money,
    would kiss him if he let me,

and then go home to my husband,
  and tell him, *I like the new salon,*
  but in our bedroom I hide the bag
  with the shampoo, curl activator, and everything else
  I will rub in my palms,
  apply to my head, every day until I can go back,
  spend a little more,
  hoping the husband won't find it,
  knowing he will,
  knowing he'll forgive me my desperation,
  this lapse in judgment,

and he'll say, *you always look beautiful to me*,
     and I'll smile with gratitude,
     and won't tell him
     how that's just not enough.

THIS IS NOT AN AUDITION

I was auditioning for The Wizard of Oz,
       and you know what part I wanted.
       The other actors,   my friends,
       kept mentioning my wild hair,
       grown wilder   as I've aged,
       my fierce mouth, the extent to which
       you can always see my teeth.

But I want to be Dorothy, I whined, and soon,
       we were on stage,   being judged,
       and the director kept nodding
       and smiling and whispering—
       you know where this is going—
       and I knew what role they thought best
       for me, and yes,   it suddenly made sense.

I've worked hard to be both wicked and illicit,
       always on the edge of my own
       dying, a flame near its wick, the wax
       spilling over and ruining everything.

Everything will be wrecked   in the end;
       burn me well
       or drown me now,   please.

ARROGANCE

My village wasn't slashed and burned today,
        and since I don't live in a village,
        all I had was guilt
        which seems to wash over the coast of Jersey
        now and then like a red algae swarm
        or the predicted high tides
        said to imperil our future.   I live on a cul-de-sac

        which seems like a French word for a circle
        of homes, but there is no such word in that language

though they have a coast, too, and, I'm sure, epidemics
        of guilt, but today there's only the one I have
        that these pills won't assuage.

And next door, I hear screaming.   The neighbor's
        son is home from Iraq,
        his teen girlfriend is pregnant,
        and the mother-in-law has Alzheimer's.

None of this was on the news,
        and my children are playing quietly, for once, with clay.
One is making pizza; the other a princess crown.

I stand by the window watching the weather
        creep in from across the bay.   Some foreign
        smell is in it;
        something I don't care to know about;
        something I wouldn't dare to claim.

EVANESCENCE

She accused of me of being heterosexist,
     but I swear I'm only heterocentrist,
     the center of my wheel
     a place that likes to be spoked,
     undoubtedly, flaming heterosexual,
     out and proud, shame only for those who,
     well, get their kicks out of shame.

But she means it, and I think she thinks her borders
     outside the margin aren't mine
     or that I stand in some other howling margin
     declaiming like a new feminist
     with avante garde death theories
     about both poems and poems about women
     sidling up to the dangerous beast of heat and shame,
     which is, frankly, the hottest place to be in this cold, cold world,

where women like the two of us,
     at our ages, whether we have lovers or not,
     are unseen by the young passersby
     who don't even wonder
     why we are suddenly and so gloriously
     yelling at each other,
     and just keep on moving by.

LIGHTER

The man in the car next to me was shaving,
  and I wanted to yell
  post-avant-this, not at him, but at the camera
  posted just over the traffic light
  we were both sitting below.

We know we're being watched, but do our best
  to live as if we're not,   but here,
  on a bright autumn morning
  I forgave him his grooming,
  applauded his time saving measures.

Maybe he'd spent the night with a new lover
  (I liked this idea) or helped his kid
  finish the science project (my sympathy grew)
  or maybe he does this every day,
  preferring all the sleep he can get
  to a few dead minutes staring in a mirror
  with a sharp blade.

Who couldn't love a man like that?

He was looking at himself in the rear-view,
  his neck exposed for me, voyeur
  in the next lane,   the eye in the sky
  witness to what was in my face,
  how I hoped to hold on to whatever
  this was for the rest of the day,
  paying a little of it out,
  keeping most of it for myself.

It was small,
      a paring knife with an inward curve
      on the back end as if for a thumb.
We both admired
      its beauty and utility,
      though it was clear neither of us
      fully understood it.
I opened some cheese and used the tip to tip it
      out onto a white triangular plate,
      and then to slip a crescent onto a cracker
      and handed it to him.

Good cheese, he said.

Neither of us smiled.

In the other room a party was going on
      we didn't want to join.   Instead, we waited
         for the doves (beating, beating) that always enter
            a room if you wait long enough,
      the things waiting to be said:
         I don't like where I live.
         I miss my sons.
         I can't leave because the money's too good.
         We're all going to die.

         Which made us laugh,

and we let our bones fall to the floor
      with us around them,
      and patted the new dog, stroking her long ears,
      the fur seeming like something
      we'd lost and won't ever get back,

      let our hands touch
      if they happened to touch
      and mumbled in our separate languages
      to the dog.

A KIND OF APOLOGY

Once in a Chinese restaurant, waiting for my dumplings,
        I noticed the wallpaper was joined
        at all the seams with staples.
From the chair molding to the ceiling, thousands of them,
        and as I looked around,
        I could see the glint where each panel met,
        the tall line of staples every few feet.

Who thought of that?
        and then held a stapler open and flat to the wall,
        moving it a millimeter at a time,
        slamming the palm of a hand
        against it to force the small metal
        into the wall board?
        Had gone around the room with a ladder,
        the time, the patience, their fat red hand
        when they were done, and why?

I thought of you
        with your tool belt finding solutions to problems
        or problems for solutions,
        and then my dumplings came.

They were hot.
        I slipped them whole
                into my mouth
                        one at a time.
I ate them all
        and asked for more.

THE CAVE

I could not go to jail,
       so I had five children,
       and when that wasn't enough, animals,
       and students, liking best the trainable and sturdy kind,
       the somewhat wild ones,
       those that could be reasoned with.
       It is necessary to know your prison,
       or to manufacture one because without it,
       there is nothing to resist.   Oddly,
       my marriage is not the confinement
       it is for so many, for me like shopping
       with a pocket full of cash;
       I want for nothing.   Nothing
       is withheld, and so I do not write love poems
       because all I can say is
               Yes, the beloved, and *How lucky am I?*

But there is this cave called time
       that we all live in.

It begins here.   It ends there.

This is the revolver to my head,
       always,
       and why I hold hostages against the fortunes.

How can you be rich unless you are willing
       to steal everything you can manage?

And when I go, bury me in the yard
       with the dog and play
              that score from Lawrence of Arabia.

Name the trees again for me,
       and then if you can, forget them.

II

DANDELIONS

SO DOES SHE GET THE DOG OR NOT?

I'm thinking of getting a dog.
It's been eight years since Bailey died;
I might be over that lolled black tongue enough
       to risk loss again.
Of course, everyone loves dogs.

I knew a man once, the local sheriff,
       who took two weeks off
       when his shepherd died.
Last night my daughter said her macncheese
       tasted like wet dog,
       and I knew what she meant.

Everybody's had a dog die.
It's a world of betrayal, a kind of stick it to you.
But isn't that the way? On some gross consciousness level,
       my Buddhist friend would say;
       down in the subtle world,
       we're all just a one eyed dogs with three legs,
       laughing at the pain.
       I laugh at the pain! One barks,
       riding the tiger
           on the turtle
               on the rock
                   of the world.
Bet me a world,
       bet me a dog,
           one black tongue,
     one daughter,
           a bowl of yellow, oozing pasta,
     one sure thing, this *now*,
           this choosing, again;
     lay it down
           and then forget about it;
     nothing is a sure thing.

"WELL, CLARICE, HAVE THE LAMBS STOPPED SCREAMING?"

They're a fun bunch, those
     who know the worth of trash
     like my lonely Craigslist friend, offering *Everything*
     for free, free, just come haul it away; it's all for free,
     just for you, if you'll call me, please. Please call.

Or the one offering twelve "mature" hydrangea bushes,
     You dig and haul; don't email me, I won't respond,
     just come with your truck and a pal;
     don't knock on my door, I won't help,
     but don't pass up this great opportunity;

     Or *My trash is your treasure; come go*
     through my basement with me little girlie.

     Or today: *Free 12 year old beagle: come clean his puke*
     off my kitchen floor and he's all yours.

It used to be we'd stroll the Galloway Saturday morning
     flea market before people carried their coffee
     in super sized cups, before people stopped being
     dazzled by what's possible to be found and bought
     for just a few dollars, delight costing little,

before Antiques Road Show
     made us imagine we horded the value
     of somebody's entire college degree
     in our attics,   before we wanted to bank
     on that chair Uncle George hauled
     from house to house because he loved
     the curve of its legs, how it made his spine
     tingle because it echoed the shape of his spine,
     and now it's our chair,
     and we want it caressed by twin appraisers
     who will ooh and aaah and tell us
     it will buy, at least, that cheap condo
     in Florida we hoped for, especially now

that the housing bubble has burst,
that bubble not about glory,
but greed;   oh, I've turned

this poem into one of grievance
          not grief, the kind I might actually feel
          if I answer that Craigslist ad about all the free stuff
          and went to that person's basement in Keyport, NJ
          descended into it, not thinking
          of *Silence of the Lambs*
          or of Dhamer   or wondering
          if I might be padlocked into a cell
          and left to die and rot into someone's great idea
          for a screenplay,   like SAW/HOSTEL 52—
          what is 52 in Roman Letters anyway—
          but once again my bad case of irony and disaffection
          distracts me from that basement
          in the little un-glorious Jersey Shore town
          nothing like Asbury or Wildwood or Atlantic City
          to elevate it,   just people, mostly trash
          Irish like me,   all *American Dream*
          and living by the ocean,
          making some kind of living
          that gets you through the winter,
                    wet spring, humid summer, the glorious fall;
          yes, nothing really like fall
          at the Jersey Shore, all warm water and no tourists,
          so the beaches are pretty empty,

and just up the road, Sandy Hook,
          Gateway National Recreation Area
          with free entrance, but pay for parking,
                    and out there   a nudist beach,
                              and old fort,
                              lots of birds,
                              and all for free, free, and   that doorway
                    into your basement,
that you want me
          to pass through with you, what will we find
          down there that I don't already own?

DISPENSABLE (EVERYWHERE THERE ARE MEN WHISPERING)

I am in the stands;   I understand nothing
       except   I have a son   out there.

He has his plated muscles;   me, my lap top.
The only people who speak loudly are the parents,
        the mothers especially; one is talking up a recruiter,
        hungry dog, dragging him to her husband,
        who says about his son:
        this one will be better than his brothers,
        and talks Division A or Double A,
        who's offered invitations, shown early interest.

Someone thinks I am writing stats,   might spotlight their son.
They speak to me with suspicion   and hope.

A man leads the liturgy:

        Do you want to play football?   *Yes sir!*
        Do you want to play football?   *Yes sir!*
        Will you work hard?   *Yes sir.*
        Louder.   *Yes sir!*
        Say Hard work!   *HARD WORK!*
        Again.   *HARD WORK!*
        You gotta focus. You gotta want it.
        You gotta focus. Say it!   *FOCUS!*
        Don't let anybody take it away from you.
        Persevere. Say it!   PERSEVERE!

The boys are kneeling.   The man walking
        among them believes
        he is saving their lives.

I understand nothing.   Tell me

    what to say to my son,
        yelling *nigga, come and get me,*
        yelling *Spartans, prepare for glory,*
        yelling *pain is only weakness leaving this body,*

his body like a ball soaring over the green of this unspeakable world.

THEY DREAM OF AK47S

There is only a hunting rifle,
        and the hunting club of lower middle class men
        in the lower half of NJ, yet I wish to speak
        of the Kalashnikov, named after its Russian inventor,
        but who cares about that? Certainly not these men
        who have brought their boys to the club,
        (and my own, whose name is Hunter),
        and have left them there in this school for boys.

Hunter tells me that some of the men
        are professionals, lawyers, VPs for corporations
        and others are tradesmen, work
        for the first group: build decks, fix plumbing.

Hunter tells me what he sees go on between
        these men from different worlds
        in this world, and I am proud he can speak
        with all of them, cross boundaries,
        of his affability, what some would call street smarts
        though this is the woods, and he is just twelve.

Which is only one reason why
        when I pick him up one day, and he tells me
        how one of his friends
        took his father's rifle
        and inserted it in the ass of a dead deer
        and pulled the trigger
        to see what buckshot can do,

I think of cats, women, the cave everyone wants to enter,
        the need for damage   dropped frogs,
        boys told not to cry like a girl,
        of the different kinds of hunger,   of the body

of a dead deer not yet bloated,
of William Stafford's inevitable push
off the road of that mother deer,
his surrender to what is doomed
and unsaveable,   of

            the inadequacy of   language,
                                    poems,
                    do I have to say mothers?

And I think of another poet, Tony, wanting to punch someone
            in the mouth for the sake of the Lawrences
            of the world; that irony;   and of my friends
            who tell me to take out the references to poems
            in my poems, excise the poets.   By god,
            this is my gun into the ass of America, my only buckshot.
            Would they leave me weaponless?

For his birthday, I give Hunter money;
I give him gift cards as he wanted;
I give him *Fishing the Backwash* by Jack Driscoll
            which he didn't want.

Then, on his twenty-first birthday,
            Hunter reads one of Jack's poems out loud.

I ask him what he thinks of it,
            but he refuses to comment,   silence
            another weapon
            he's learned how to shoot.

Everyday, I tell Hunter I love him.
Everyday, he says, *Hush Ma, I know.*

AT THE COMBINE: THRESHING

The agricultural harvester, the combine,
      changed the nature of farming,
      and the metaphor holds true: the beating,
      the separation of seeds from grain,
      plant from ground is similar:
           boys from men
           men from athletes
           average from stellar.
                How this field, this stadium, these boys
        wait for whatever blood they can get,
      and its seems today the sun is able to forgive anything,
      burn off the decaying smell of the world,

and my son—glorious in his 40 yard dash,
      shirt black with sweat—will be O-line MVP today.

I cheer, but am thinking of a story about a woman in Guinea
that ends with a Kalashnikov inserted in her vagina.
A boy fired it.

To fire is a metaphor that reminds us
      once gunpowder had to be lit.
Thinking about this distracts me,
      as does the fact the oldest guns
      have been found in China,
      or the crying when I visited Gettysburg once,
      only once, and never again,
      or even that the soldiers in Guinea
      smoke *brown-brown*,
      a mixture of cocaine and gunpowder.

A boy inserted it.   And fired.
Nothing particularly surprising nor moving.
He was fucked up,
      and it was just another violent day in a sports stadium,

and I am sitting in the bleachers on a warm spring day
         the leaves around me bright and singing
         their new songs; below me, there is a rustling,
         small animals or just birds. Trees seem to rush up
         behind me; the leaves are so close to my face,
         they tickle in the slightest breeze.
I am on the edge here.   Only this ringing
         aluminum stand keeps me from falling into the hole
         below me: that wide maw of a woman's spread legs.
I think I do not care about her, but about how the boy—
         for it was surely a boy holding the technological advancement
         of hand weaponry—could do this
         and of the hydrostatic shock that may have killed her,
         the shift in the liquids of the brain after an impact
         anywhere in the body.   But I do care
         because then I think—
                  if this can be called thinking—
         that the story began as she lay there,
         her abdomen erupted, bleeding into the earth,
         the life of her weeping
         out and staining the dirt black-black,
         and of how I have cupped my own blood
         pouringfrom between my legs after birth,
         after sex, and still, this late in my life,
         after forgetting about my period, the shock
         of it always, the warm, clotting mess
         of my own alive-ness, alive,
         but so damned baffled about it all,

even now watching these assembled boys
         at the football combine, how they leap and bray,
         run and shuttle,
         dash and bench press,

how they want it so badly,
         how their stats are collected,

how they are sorted and rated,
         scored and ranked.

YOU MAY THINK I AM SUGGESTING WOMEN ARE "THE GENTLER SEX"

Once my ex-husband told me
      he broke a kid's leg in a game.
He was proud,   he said, and not ashamed to admit it.

There's no one to blame
      for how I was hoodwinked, swallowed
      whole every myth
      of safety though fairytales are full
      of pillage and plunder.

            Yesterday,
a woman lined up twelve brown men
      in a sandy land,
            and made them put their bodies
against each other's, in a dog pile,
      heads hooded,
      in the heat and stink,
            and bruises and lost languages,   permission in
            what is implied:
            this is your ticket out, your tour of proving.

            Now, the boys
are lining up behind the coach
      whose wife is working this weekend;
            You gotta take the kid.
He holds a small boy,
      no more than a baby really,
      and exhorts the boys to
      Hit em hard and
      Go out there and put some hurt on.

They line up one to one.   They do not shyly
      bow their heads.

Lead with your shoulder, he says,
but the boys know this is a lie,
know what they must do
> if they want to win,
> want to come out on top.

LIKE WATER ON PAVEMENT

I was stalking my boys on Facebook,
    creeping, as they say, watching for phrases
    like *She's so fetch*,
    and the *Bangbros coming to a field near you*,
    or maybe just *Work sucks* by the oldest,

and their photos: so many blonde girls in two pieces,
    guns,
    tattoos,
    beer and sloppy smiles

reminding me of the sloppy smiles of their babyhoods.

Then, I smelled it before hearing it,
    knew it before seeing it:
my back to the window,
    face bent to the screen,
    wet asphalt awakens my brain,
    molecules of something I can't name released,
    entering me first through the open window,
    then my nostrils,
    the asphalt giving something of itself up,

and there's a second of relief after this hot summer,
    a moment, maybe of something like joy,
    where I consider running out into it,
    still in pajamas,
    arms in the air,
    face lifted to what I wish I could enter,
    letting it penetrate me a little,
    my eyelashes starring as if I were a girl
    in the first throws of wet and hot,

but I don't;   I bend closer,   see the pinpointed pupil
    of my boy drunk at a party,
    his face   a face   tattooed on my dying skin,

that dark point a pathway
to a universe I don't yet know,
and if I am lucky, might someday,

but for now, there is just this rain   and this technology
          that helps me go on,   everything running
          through the fingers of my open hand,   flowing
          away   like water on pavement,
          each droplet   like a node   in a social network,
          both about coalescence
          of self into other.   Does rain love the cloud it falls from?

No.   There, watch that silver trail   of drops searching
          for the river it will become.   And my son, Luke,
          is growing a beard.   And my son, Hunter, see his bones
          widening into those of a man's.   And my son, Ethan,
          in his sleeveless T, arms raised and curled, the caption:

                    These guns are cocked.   Here, let me show you

                    his recent mobile upload.

AND SOME JOIN THE MILITARY

The soldier poet recalls,
      [in the open wound the sun's breath on his lover's neck is,
      the clavicle a place to build a tent and crawl inside]

              Howling sand   vegetable   swamp
              humid-less here   pea green air there
              and air traffic stopped today
              due to volcanic ash!
              Yesterday   last week   the week before
              and before, it was a body in the wheel well,
              and how silly we think! Ash circling the globe,
              and the cruises canceled because the flights
              with the tourists couldn't arrive,

and says, *Here is where the world ends.*
He carries a dead limb, alive with image,
      not in a bag, but in his arms like a baby
      he will someday have,

                        like the father
      who has survived fifteen years
      of shaking recollection of his son's near
      death in that bombing
          (oh, it doesn't matter which one; if you've forgotten,
          there is sure to be another one)
      at that event at the high school
      in some town in South Dakota—
      whisper it and it sounds like every high school
      in America.   Somewhere,

      there is a boy finding his way out
      of something in the small, open faced grin
      of a another boy in uniform who scored
      high marks in people skills, in his ability
      to convince, cajole, get close to, and close the deal.

He doesn't carry a gun, he doesn't have to,
     and it might seem cheap to say he does
     just as much damage when he promises
     the other boys, and sometimes girls,
     that they will carry a gun,

            a big, fucking, blaster,
                of a fucking amazing gun
            that can blow   *blow*   *blow*
            the fucking commies
               gooks roaches   sand fleas
krauts-teachers-other-other-other-other muthafuckas away.

And with them,
     the blown seeds already germinated
     in the new recruit's mind of *no-other-way-to-get-out*
          of this town
          or fucked up family,
          the alcoholic mother,
          or the sad, depraved one,
          or the stupid one,
          or the father with no job
   (oh, sing again James Wright
   of the terrible galloping! The suicidally beautiful!),
          or the incest or the *not-smart-enoughs*,
          or the no friggin' jobs (a thousand people
   turned out today to apply for a job at the new Applebee's
   on Washington Ave. in No Hope, Arizona,
   a thousand, and each one somebody's
   kid or father or mother with a smile and a clean shirt
   gone sweaty and grey in the hot,
   long line of *what-the-fuck-I-bother-for-anyway?*).

Read that as *I*, motherfucker.   *I*.
     I didn't get the job.
     I wasn't good enough.
     I didn't have the money.
     I got pregnant.

I got her pregnant.
I did that awful thing to the kid next door.
I dreamed of being a hockey player.
I played the video game all day.
I played so I wouldn't cry.
I burned my arm with the cigarette because I couldn't.

THERE WERE ONLY DANDELIONS

And the boy.

Everywhere, sound. Here: sirens. There: sirens.
And the crying

> [because one woman's husband
> doesn't love her anymore
> and wants to go to medical school,
> now, after so many years of lawyering;
>
> because another one woke up one day,
> told her husband, *I don't think I ever want
> to sleep with you again*, meaning sex,
> and then he learned it meant not
> even the sleeping, the spooned, belly loose
> intimacy of Howler Monkey night;
>
> because the dandelion blew
> into a million parachuting seeds.]

Pre-dandelions floating everywhere, to every continent.
There, too, screaming, just like sirens,
        and everywhere in between, each anniversary of the living.

My boy is in college now, one says,
        but that day of the bombing,
        when they called, I stopped at the 7-11
        to buy bags to bring the body parts home in.
        He was one of only four that survived.

> [Whose baby, anonymous, in the trash heap?
>
> Whose boys aiming, aiming, falling in love
> with the fear they won't ever outrun?

Whose child that one,
without an arm, a knife in the other?]

They're not all white faces, and this poem
is not a public poem.
Not all poems are meant to entertain,
like Jericho said, named
after that city by that river
in the hot place so many people
have lived in, so many hostages
been taken in, so many,
so many—whose offices I can't name or know—
no, not entertain, but sing just the same,
a polyphony of song
birds in the morning,
snow geese aflight, guns rocketing,
barrel out, sound through
the beating blood,
bleating animals, beseeching
all those river gods
for some respite from this suffering.

[Each a lawn weed having grown
up in some crevice,
against the wall of each life,
flowering heads all in all
and each in one, this explosion
on the seed headed-planet,
fractal imagining, and this
is my imagining, this declaimed *I*.]

Though some of you—
even though this is not a public poem—
will say the *I* is dead; there is no self;
no things but in ideas
dead, yet no ideas in things either;
and then the accumulation
of linguistic artifacts heats up like a
like a like a

Lava lamp.
[All Spencer's Gift's glow and thrift store chic.]

And you will not be warmed by it,
    but   who is this *you?*
    Because if there is no *I,*
    there can be no *we,*
and I am not willing to surrender to that.

    [to no *us-ness,* to you not being
    one sole being on the other end
    of this *this-ness,* but only part
    of some conglomerate, corporate
    entity called nothing-we-can-comprehend.
    I am unwilling;
    I am a dissenter.
    I *am.*]

Which renders the corporation something
    more than *they,*
    which is almost always paralytic or amoral,
    certainly unsympathetic and unsympathizable,
    something   approaching   evil.

Just you.   And me.   Please.

First, I claim this *I,* that only has this
    language(s), technology(s),   space,
        time,   sex,   gender,   religion
            or lack thereof,
            sensibility,   sense,
                a body,   a body in time,
                    in sex, in faith and betrayal
                        and reason and reasoning:

out of this great unsynthesized manifold,
    all penetration and penetrating.

[Like a seed head blown apart,
all pollination and flowering
and dried and falling away
and lifting and airborne and borne
away from each other to land
and germinate and survive
in the meagerness of conditions,
the little dying, the little survivals.]

An image, Williams said; an idea, said Stevens,
        ancestors we think of: lion's teeth leaves, prickly
        and persevering, no things but in ideas, really?

So much depends upon this small boy
        who doesn't look like any small boy you know;
He is my small boy— the *I* of this *this-ness*—
        with small bones and wide dark eyes,
        hair as straight and black as spun obsidian.
So much depends upon a child like him, this one I love,
        sitting in calf high grass, so new-green, the edges
        blaze white, and the dandelions all sprung over night,
        one night in this boy's newborn awareness,
        as new as any child's, burying his face in the common
        and undervalued florets, eyes blazing with YELLOW!!
        Mind cracking—everywhere this cracking—a portal
        into a new way of being, the dancing around him,
        the buzz of new insects, the spray of misting winds;

it is all so amazing, this world of wonder.

YOU MIGHT SAY THIS IS NOT A POEM

We are in each others' manifolds, like those celebrities
      who enter dreams at night, Quentin Tarantino
      closer to you then, say, your neighbor, a no-brainer,
      but maybe also your father? I could stand my own
      father's insanities better if he was QT or dead Patrick Swayze
      or Oprah, for god's sake. What would Chuck Palahniuk
      say if he spoke to you in a dream?

And those who resist
      the poets who will come and go in this poem,
      why do you want them held at such remove
      from the real action? Would we be better off
      discussing an episode of CSI? Or the crassness
      of movies like SAW or HOSTEL or why we
      need so badly to popularize our fears, march them
      out of the dark like clowns, see them beaten bloody:
            torture and the torturers, our own complicity.

Oh god, let me have the poets, please.

Like Jerry, union leader and poet,
      in this age of dismantlement:
      unions, culture-rage at the educators,
      new American Jewery, ghettoized and vilified;
      why can't we be like Jerry? Book
      in pocket, sign in hand, stand
      for something. Say *I stand*
      for something! Instead, we revive
      super heroes: Cancer Girl! Strikes in Pink!
      Kick Ass! Kids can kill! Kill Bill!
      Atwood's angry women, victims
      always becoming victimizers;
      think Liberia, think South Africa,
      think your Uncle George,
      years in that orphanage in Jersey City,
      and the undoing, undermining

of what can be born in a yard of dirt
with a stick and common yellow-headed
weeds, some water, the teeming of ants,
oh that glory:
a small boy's frog under the rock,
that self-mirror of the civilized
and the wild in each of us
under that next upturned
gray-blue speckled slate on the edge
of a moving body of water,
and what gets born in the interweaves
between a self (someone's burgeoning fragile *I*!)
and nature,
that silly word, almost as silly as *they*.

Bringhurst said *Everywhere being is dancing.*

That buzz beneath it all, beneath us all, that voice
        behind your mind, that child-knowing,
        and then the grief,
        the self-loathing, the reduction of *I*
        to only a member
        of a group
        (family, classroom, religion, culture, this nation, that),
                ketchup sandwiches,
                        cruelty in numbers,
                                numbers of children without

        what Bringhurst was talking about.

You might say you do not wish to be in my poem.
You are. And feel free to include me in yours.

SATURATION

Intensity! Oh, immutable hue, do not assert yourself.
Why, even gray has differences in lightness or brightness,
       and who lives in anything less than vividness? Too many,
       the world a soft haze like most New Jersey spring days,
       cast in a toxic glow, air heavy with fine particulates
       and locked moisture that can't go up or down;
       The balance of our own internal eco-systems tilted,
       everyone a little anxious, wanting to get drunk,
       go to sleep, or fuck someone up, bad, not unlike burning
       your arm with a cigarette to see if you're still alive
       inside all the murk. Murky water, dark wall paint,
       the VOCs eating out your brainstem with each stroke
       of Sherwin Williams, no lead anymore—another generation's
       poison—and now the low-VOC paint, just more expensive.

It's always more expensive to live safely.
And impossible,   but we try.

Like TV, that cliché of self-medication.

Today a student said *I don't watch TV; I only watch wrestling.*
Another said, *I don't watch it either; I only watch Reality TV.*

Does anyone   howl anymore?   About anything?
Oh, Corso! Oh, Ginsberg!
Oh, Patti Smith at his knee
     all elbow and jawbone
         and hair-product–less hair singing
             Frederick, not afraid to say *name of care*
                night of wonder
                   wings of a dove,
     yes, scream, dance, fuck, sing,
     call the sky
     a neo-fantastical-dream-of flight,
     call on the names of those you love,
     those you've betrayed;

paint the sky with the forgiveness you owe,
   punch a hole through this saturated life
   and step right through.

THE DOG IS LYING ON THE FLOOR
AS I WRITE THIS

The dog will be a recurrent actor in this story.
        The story of *I* in relation.
            One of those relations is the dog.

I am not a dog person.
        Some people are.   They proclaim
            this as if it indicates the club they belong to.
            It is almost a racial or religious declaration:
                oh, yeah, I'm a dog person.
        No yellow star. No dark skin, but they are different.

I am not a dog person.
        I have a cat, too, but I am not a cat person, either,
            and I resist the pressure to choose
                or to explain myself.

My dog is named Flannery. You know why
        and you will either like me for that or snicker.
        I don't care. She lays at my feet when I write,
        not at yours.
        You can go fuck yourself
        if you don't like my dog's name.

My dog is MY dog.
        She is not the family dog,
            although she is the family's dog.
Whether I am a good dog owner or bad,
        Flannery has bonded with me. And I her.
I don't mind her vomit
        as much as I have minded other dogs' vomit.
Or feces. I pick up her warm bowel movements in a bag.
I am not alone in this.
It does not mark me as a good person—
        nor as a dog person—many people do this.
           It may even be the law in some places.

I do sympathize with her brown eyes
    that seem badly to want
        to understand
            and surely wish to please.

And how she follows me around.
How she is depressed
    when I am gone,
        how she needs those dog bones
            and the chewing.   I empathize,
with that:
        how many vodkas? Bags of potato chips?
        Other things it's none of your business to know
            I have consumed, used, interfaced with
                in the same desperate anxiousness?

Some people would save an animal before a human.
    I am not that kind of person.
        I would eat an animal,
        no problem, to save myself.
        I would throw an animal
        over a bridge to save my child.

    I knew a girl once
        who was given a box of kittens
        by a nun at the convent
        a few blocks from my house,
        told to take it down to the creek
        by the library and put some rocks in the box
        and drop it off the bridge.

I don't know who I would be
    if someone had ever asked me
        to do something like that.

I don't know what that girl actually did.

I did see a man cut the testicles off a young pig once.
     I was holding the pig.
          He threw the testicles to the ground,
              said the barn cats would get them.

We raised that pig, had it butchered, and ate it.   Bacon.

But dog? In "The Art of Living" by John Gardner
     a cook kills a dog and makes a sumptuous meal.
     It is an initiation story, a loss of innocence,
     a boy becomes a man. Not through sex,
     though there is a girl, but by seeing through time.

Dog time is my time.   It is child-time:
     now.   Always now.

Seeing the past and the future is how we suffer,
     the bones we gnaw on, endlessly.

The smell of bacon always seducing us.

III

THE DOOR

THEN THE PANIC WAS THROUGH

And we were all afraid of winter,
      the one that kept coming,
      the circling around storms,
      out over the coast
      then back over the mainland,
      dropping snow like bombs,
      innocuous as that:
            wet galumphing balloon snow
                  dropping on our heads
                        from a school-boy god,

      and so many that winter,

and how I loved the long lines
      in the ShopRite and Acme,
      the Foodtown and WalMart,
      the sweet local mart, Sickles,
      with its fine cheeses one just
      can't live without
      if snowed in for days.

I loved the way people would argue
      if someone cut ahead,
      or a new line suddenly opened,
      and when the power went out
      in the A&P for a few minutes,
      so the cash machines
      had to recalibrate, we were all
      getting hungry and tired,
      and the woman with the crutches
      cursed at the man with the sick child
      who had sneezed on her back,
      and all of our faces were gray skies
      ready to burst,

the big windows to the world
covered in sales announcements:
      canned peas, ten for a dollar!
      Bryers Ice Cream, two for the price of one!

And then we were outside,
      laughing as we went to our cars,
      handing over carts to people just arriving,
      already forgetting which storm this was,
      or how many had come before, not wondering
      if we'd make it to spring, just sick to death
      inside our coats and cars,
      our fists full of cookies and Slim Jims.

THOSE THINGS OUTSIDE

The Trees.
Those things outside with roots.
A little conversation with them
  is all I ask. Well, not really all,
  but something and many times over.

On my lawn there is one, a giant swamp Ash,
  with seven trunks. I've named them all,

but the tree does not care;
  trees do not respond to names,
  only to sunlight,
  and I do not speak that language.

Only those things with roots speak
  in the burbling silences of push and gather
  in the confluence of atmosphere and matter.

But I try. With my back against the bark,
  spine to spine, my little bones align
  and the horizontality of my life slips vertical.
And old;
  from here to there, who can imagine that?
All that below us? So much beyond?

  Sometimes,
I speak the language of soil,
  or its poor cousin, dirt.
I imagine the dialect of rock,
  but am a poor communicator with nature.
Once, I thought I knew how,
  thought a whale off the coast
  of Massachusetts told me to listen,
  and I did. For a long time,
I could hear it from miles away,
  and let me tell you, that was a hopeful thing.

In the big waters, things move;
    they don't have roots.
Over the surface of the earth, animals move;
in the air, who really knows what navigates there?

,

TO THE GOD OF PYROGRAPHY

It's not a public panic like it used to be—
      then, we simply said,
      maybe we'll only lose a child or two,
      or some old people; now we are older
      and those children are ours,
      and we might even be the old,
      the infirm, the ones to be culled—
      now it's a quiet fear, more personal.
      No one is talking
      about it and we have agreed
      that there's nothing to be done,
      but wait it out, again.

Like bad weather.   Listen, there's a howling

      in among the trees. The beautiful old ones
      our taxes pay to keep;
      out in the public park with the thousand tulips
      that bloom each spring;
      the one with the once new, now old
      arsenic laced playground
      that has all of our names on it,
      burned into each wooden slat,
      Martin Family here,   Graber family there.

A long time ago, we gathered
      for a winter solstice bonfire,
      burning wood
      kissing in the dark
      drinking something   hot.

We don't go out in the dark anymore;
      what burns there isn't wood,
      and we're not willing
      to sacrifice anything.

      Not one damned thing.

RIVER, STICK, BONE

I watched the brothers slow dance
      with their backs to each other,
      hands like sea creatures
      surviving between the sun and moon
      of their faces.
One had a hat,
      the other, a pretty handkerchief.
That's a word you don't see much anymore,
      and the word flowered from his breast pocket
      and crawled along the crease
      of his jacket
      to hide
      in another pocket,
      and his brother's hat spelled out
A river is an unclosed fist.
[Some things you can't write poems about;
Some things just have to be endured.]
And these brothers are in love
      like lovers are in love
      and love words like lovers
      don't need them,
      adoration and endurance
      twin words who love each other,
      who offer refuge, respite from the other,
      a little hideaway
      for those secrets
      that enlarge us all.
Between the sun and moon
      is a dark ocean
      where all rivers collude,
      a confluence of stick and bone.

For Andre

THE SINS

Of the father, he says.
Yes, I've heard that. Read that. Mothers, I think.
Just that one word.
Passed down, he says. *What we have to bear; what we repeat.*

I want to ask, did your mother love you?
But I don't.
I ask, *did you feel loved by your mother,*
　　　and he tilts his head slightly to the left,
　　　his mouth opening just a bit, too,
　　　so I can see his moist, shiny teeth.
　　　I won't tell you what he told me;
　　　every man's mother is his secret love,
　　　and to share it would be another kind of betrayal.

He told me I was beautiful,
　　　but I refused to look at him as he said it,
　　　knowing motherhood includes
　　　ignoring errors　　　sometimes,
　　　letting the sins of those we love
　　　transpire　　　pass through us,
　　　the desire of men
　　　not to be held accountable
　　　for every last thing.

WHAT FOOLISHNESS

The fall my ex-husband had the heart attack,
    my cousin lost her breasts
    and gained a year of chemo,
    and my step mom had that mass
    on her lung removed,
    you kept telling me I looked good
    in that video.

That was the same fall the traffic
    light in town started having a left turn
    arrow some hours of the day and not others.

After the first accident,
    the mayor said the notice
    in the town newsletter
    should have been enough warning,
    and if only more of his constituents
    would read it,
    we'd all be better off.

That was when I thought of this as a town,
    a word that has such a friendly sound,
    and when I thought I had a family,
    which sounds so permanent,
    and when people started dying,
    and leaving in all the ways people do:
    college, military, marriage,
    you were there telling me
    I could increase my website hits easily,
    and that I could, if I wished, share
    my extensive knowledge of this world
    with the world
    as long as I understood it
    would be fact-checked by you,
    or someone designated by you.

When I thought I was losing the baby,
  it was you I turned to, and, to your credit,
  you stood by me,
  never judging, just giving me the facts
  and many thoughtful opinions.

That fall, as I sat nearly paralyzed
  at the window watching another rainstorm
  forcing the leaves off my trees,
  you sat on my lap, and I felt less alone.

But those leaves, those leaves,
  and so many rainstorms that fall,
  so odd, one after the other like that,
  and my poor trees, how just as they reached
  good color were stripped bare.

QUEERNESS MEANS QUESTIONING
THE MYTHICAL NORMS

Must we ourselves not become gods simply to appear worthy…?
NIETZSCHE

Listen to the breathless carrying on,
  one choral group after another,
  the harmonies, librettos, musical scores,
  and something like god stirs in the guts.

What we need is a queer god,
  not Republican queer, all self-loathing and denial,
  but queer as the top-sizing of Moby Dick,
  of Jesus as black-skinned,
       Trans or, better, Intersexed, and singing
  like a black throated swan,
  all snorkeling croak,
  surprising in his her-ness,
  or she wearing a man's tux.

Oh, sing choral groups; oh, soldier on
  you stained glass makers;
oh, rich, get as rich as you want;
  thinkers think;
       cooks cook;
       run mad with word processing you poets:
       question everything;
       believe in nothing,
       everything we design gets away from us.

FOMENTATION

Today, it is snowing again
and somewhere Jerry turns 85,
      sure to be gnarling a girl's sweatered forearm
      between his meaty hands,
      snorting about how beautiful it all is
      and reading some of Lucille's living poems
      celebrating every day that didn't kill her—
      now that she is gone, and the person

    who is wearing the sweater,
    who hates the cold,
    who is young and maybe uncertain
    and as yet un-authorial
    and maybe even a little, for now, lazy
    and dazed, wanting only to slip
    off that sweater and scour their skin
    with the skin of someone else,
        will feel those bone-fingers,
        those knuckle gems,
        those hands that have rubbed
        the spines
        of thousands of books
        and kneaded the bread
        of his own rising,
        will feel the small warm cave
        inside themselves
        and a part of them will uncurl into it,
        engage the dark funk of her own-ness

as Jerry chortles, *Memory is dangerous.*

    It's only in the caves and the patches
    of fragrant weed and the wasted things
    that one can think
        and roam inside the boney bag
        we all become, but together,

in the walking out
or the lying in,
the moving through,
the seeing and the listening,
the eating and the drinking, we are
an insurrection.

GOD ON THE ROPES

There must be those among whom we can sit down and weep and still be
counted as warriors.   ADRIENNE RICH

Kama sits on the bench,
      his feet smelling of grease,
      a bag of peanuts for the squirrels
      who won't come too near
      for fear of the bees
      on his wilting bowstring.

Oh, he looks a fright.
Not even the cops will come close,
      afraid of a shot to the heart,
      what love-struck can do to a man,
      not enough sick time in the world to recover,
      afraid they'd put down their tasers
      and take up singing the Blues. They stand

      nearby, erect on their horses,
      almost guarding him,
      Kama's parrot shifting from one foot to the other,
      pecking at the bees,
      wanting them orderly,
      wanting Kama to ride him, wanting
      to spear lovers, but there's nothing doing,

      just these damned
      squirrels skirting between the trees,
      their tiny squeaks betraying their desire,
      and the horses' nostrils blowing sympathetic steam
      while Kama shifts his feet back and forth
      like any god might do,
          impatient,
              impotent, not omni-,
                    out to pasture,
      sting-less, and uninsured.

KNOWLEDGE

i keep hearing / tree talk / water words / and i keep knowing what they mean.
LUCILLE CLIFTON

Some streets are better than others,
  but there are trees everywhere.
  Kathy doesn't notice the trees,
  only the dogs,
  but Marc can talk about them
  as if they were old friends,
  as if the town were inhabited
  only by things with roots.
I watch Kathy's eyes as they follow
  the young men who follow her;
  it's uncertain which one is analogous to dog,
  who is leader, who is being led,
  but they love her like young pups,
  and frolic with her at the train station,
  spreading and unashamed,
  showing her their tattoos and hidden poetry.
  Her eyes go wide.

Marc, on the other hand, only holds out small plants
  he grows in his office overlooking the station:
  you can't see in or out for the foliage.

Those boys are carving
  their names into tree trunks again,
  and Marc is leading a walk among the trees.

It's February; the world is silver
  and the trees,
    some hundreds of feet tall,
  look like the Silver Splashers
  at the YMCA in town,
  all glorious spindle and arc,

arms hanging over the roadway,
nothing ashamed about them,
and proud of their scars.

They beckon to everyone in their silent manner.

PROGENITORS OF THE NEW WHALE

Last night at the gym,
      I took Bob into the sauna with me,
      dragging him not kicking or screaming,
      but smoldering into the heat
      where I couldn't break a sweat.

I was paralyzed and so was he,
      peering out the glass door
      as if someone would show
      up any moment.

I was reading Moby Dick
      and Bob was reading the Bible backwards—
      oh, you thought I was reading Bob,
      and the Melville comment threw you off,
      but what is literal? What is figurative?

Bob was in the interstices,
      between the molecules collected
      on my skin from the exertion
      of exercising my mind, and now, I watched
      him paging through the Bible,
      looking for the lost narratives
      under the meta-narrative,
      the truth not in the word, but in the world,
      and I turned Moby Dick upside down,

and Bob said, *cool*, and laughed. When we tried to leave,
      the door was stuck,
      and I started to panic. Bob said, be *cool*,
      and now it wasn't so funny,   and he beckoned
      below the benches to a man I hadn't known

was there, and out crawled Rilke
who knelt
and let Bob climb on his shoulders.

He peeled
        back the cedar lining the ceiling,
        pushing up the tiles,
        which is when I really started   to sweat,
        and when I left the gym,
        I left alone,   but unafraid.

IN PHYSICS, RADIATION DESCRIBES
ANY PROCESS IN WHICH ENERGY
TRAVELS THROUGH A MEDIUM OR
THROUGH SPACE, ULTIMATELY TO
BE ABSORBED BY ANOTHER BODY
                            — WIKIPEDIA

That's the title of my poem, which is not a public poem.
There should be no public poems,
        like going to ice hockey
                or Barnum and Bailey
                        or even Cirque du Soleil
        with its hard bodies and exploding balloon-heads
        and money from the suckers
        who think they're cooler
        than the audiences for Nascar or wrestling.

I think I don't want poems like cans of beer
        but like reliquaries;
        Poems like the teeth of the dead in catacombs.
        Like the thousand year old vines growing at Ankor Wat.

This is not an ars poetica; it's a plea to fund research
        for space travel,
        pay for art programs,
        pray for rain in hot places,
        and new stove technology in all third world countries.

I want poems like a cure for malaria;
        poems in the chemo bag at the chemo café
        where the cancer patients line up like people
        with tickets to the circus.   Give me poems
        like radiation tattoos: breast, rib.
        I know someone who had anus cancer:
                think face down, ass up; don't tell me
                that doesn't suck;
                don't tell me that isn't funny.

I want poems like that: energy passing through space
      absorbed by another body.
          To save her life
              by almost killing her first.
So we can sit on the porch   and have a few
      beers, toast each other, find a way
          to go on.

WHAT REALLY DIES IN AUTUMN

In a bar somewhere
     during an ordinary October, a former husband
     sits with his former wife,
     and they talk about the son they share.
     The husband tells her how proud he is of the boy,
     how great football is: the loyalty
          to teammates, willingness to work through pain,
          leadership by men of boys
          who want to become men,   and she
goes quiet, sensing her ex has slid into the memory
     of his own high school games. He is so specific,
recalling yardage and names.
          He is embarrassed
with emotion and shrugs
     like he used to while they were married.

She sips her vodka,   content to listen
     for once   and not judge.
He sips his bourbon   and talks.

When they leave, she feels feathery,
          the small, tight ball in her chest
          that used to keep her from taking a deep breath,
          suddenly gone.   She doesn't immediately
          understand this
          as a sign of forgiveness,
but when she leaves her ex
     in the parking lot,
          an image comes to her
          of him
               as a boy
     and marvels at a strange awareness:
What would he have been like
had she been his mother
instead of his wife?

     Then:
And how else might she have failed him?

THE FLAGS WE RAISE

He that hath wife and children hath given hostages to fortune.
FRANCIS BACON

Named after his Dutch grandfather,
    Ruth, pronounced *root*,
    whose name was changed
    by an Ellis Island gatekeeper,   Rutger
    has no freckles or pale skin,
    but black on black eyes
    slanted and long-lashed,
    hair that swings with its own
    smooth-cuticled weight.

It could have been different genetically:
before the Chinese, the Dutch colonized Taiwan,
    then called Formosa, where my son was born,
    and so he could have had something
    of that other land in him,
    the genes of his adopted father,
but instead his face is round like an islander's,
    with a graceful flat nose—you'd think Polynesian
    before Chinese [that might be the biggest legacy
    the Dutch left Taiwan: encouraging Han Chinese immigration,
    and later, it seemed reasonable for China's government
    to relocate itself there.].

Today, whose land this is is still a question,

    but whose child this is is not:
    Ruth, who traded his name
    for the possibilities of this place,
    had a daughter, who had a son, my husband,
    who claimed this boy in a country that understands
    nuance and complexity in ways the West does not,

    and can also claim the way this boy
    and his mottled background changes us:

where once our ancestors
visited and stole, today—though some declaim
this is as another kind of stealing—we surrender
to a rainbow's soft demarcations into colors
outside of history or place.
When I say *Rutger*,
   I hear *Kuan Lu*.

When I say *Kuan Lu*,
   I hear *beautiful boy*.

When I say *beautiful boy*,   a flag
   is raised   in my chest
   that belongs to no country,
   but the one all hostages to fortune live in,
   one with no borders,
   which can not be escaped from,
   and of which there is no government,
   only taxes,   death,   and
   of course, what pleasures
   we can steal along the way.

SCARIFICATION

Once a nameless rigger on shore leave
      in a bar on the coast of Scotland,
      ribald with R&R after a three week
      rotation on an oil rig,
      bared his chest and waist, pointing one by one
      to his tattoos.

The last one, MOM, inked
      into the soft, moist skin inside his lower lip,
      was revealed only when he took that lip
      between thumb and fingers and peeled it down.

Drunk myself then, I think I thought:
      He has been wounded;
      he has allowed someone to pierce the membrane
      of this cavity into himself, the small cave
      of the mouth that holds secrets and cruelty,
      that kisses and spits.

I think of the rigger now as I look
      at my grown son
      asleep on the couch—
      the driving of his work days
      having exhausted him; his mother's house
      a refuge still—
      because his sleeve has lifted,
      revealing a tattoo
      of a buck's head, but also that the eyes
      have been burned out.

With a cigarette he will tell me when he wakes.

I say to my son, *How did this happen?*
      and he says, *It was intentional, Ma.*
I want to know
      if he did it

or if someone held the cigarette to his skin.
Who would do that? I whisper.

He says, *It's my body.*
He says, it is *no big deal.*
At the door,
I touch his wounded arm as though I were driving
    a concrete caisson
        into the ocean bed of his life,
    as though I could
    cap this wild, wild well before it blows.

And he steps out.

In the bar,
    my rigger flipped a coin; heads, I'd stay,
    and we'd have another drink;
    which is not what happened,
    and I left,   as people have to do.

Be careful driving, I call to my son.

He pulls his truck door closed,
    the glass opaque,
    and revs the engine
    and backs out, headlights across my lawn
    passing over me and away.

THE SMALL GOD OF WINTER, A LITTLE GOD OF TEMPERATURES

Here is the sweet old, rancid woman on the checkout line,
    with her reminder of beauty,
        the small map of her body
invisible to the young man behind her
    who hopes to discover a country

outside the dizziness of the American Mall,
    all dark chocolate,
        alligator skin boots,
            Retinol A,
                and more lingerie on parade
than any man could possibly want.

She leaves slowly, going into the bright snow-light,
    and he reaches her,   holds the door,
    but
    moves quickly beyond her   to fold himself
    into the cockpit of his tricked out
    ride   and then rides it,
    the white vapor
    of his exhaust   trailing behind.

She walks down the cold street,
    fretting about the ignorance of youth,
    the loudness of his car,
    worrying something is wrong with that damned engine,
    doesn't know steam will disappear
    while smoke lingers in the air.

Now her sinuses are sweating
    and there is a burning
    at the back of her throat;

she's unsure   which street to turn down,
    how to find her way home,

     suddenly lost in the brightness
of everything   she's old enough to know
is destructible,   a fog
where memory seems corrupt,

and the distant thrumming of a punctured muffler
is proof of a treachery she can't or refuses to recall.